Exploring the Arts

LOOKING AT PAINTINGS

by Frances Kennet
and Terry Measham

Marshall Cavendish · London · New York · Sydney · Toronto

Editorial Staff

Series Editor	Sue Lyon
Assistant Editor	Laura Buller
Art Editor	Helen James
Production Manager	Isabel Cossar
Managing Editor	Alan Ross
Editorial Consultant	Maggi McCormick

Library Edition published 1989
Published by Marshall Cavendish Corporation
147 West Merrick Road
Freeport, Long Island
N.Y. 11520

Typeset by J&L Composition Ltd,
Filey, North Yorkshire
Printed in the USA by Worzalla Publishing
Company, Wisconsin

Library of Congress Cataloging-in-Publication Data
Kennet, Frances.
   Looking at paintings/Frances Kennet and Terry Measham.
      p.   cm. — (Exploring the arts)
   Bibliography: p.
   Includes index.
   Summary. Uses several well-known paintings and suggested
activities to introduce different artists' styles and techniques and
to discuss ways to view a painting.
   ISBN 1–85435–102–8. — ISBN 1–85435–101–X (set): $85.00
   1. Painting—Juvenile literature.   2. Visual perception—Juvenile
literature.   3. Painting.   4. Visual perception.   5. Art
appreciation.   I. Measham, Terry.   II. Title.   III. Series.
ND1146.K46   1989   89–7156
750.1′1—dc20   CIP

   ISBN 1–85435–101–X (set)
   ISBN 1–85435–102–8 (vol)

Contents

Introduction

A painting is more than just a picture on the wall. A painting can make you feel happy, angry, shocked, or calm. It can teach, inform, or just entertain you. Paintings can help you to see places you may never visit, meet famous people in history, and spark your imagination with new ideas.

This book is all about enjoying paintings. How would you answer if someone asked you, "What do you think about that picture on the cover?" This book will show you how to find words to describe what you see. You will discover why an artist paints a picture, and how he brings all his ideas together on canvas.

Best of all, you will discover things about yourself and others. No one feels exactly like you do, and the way you react to pictures will be special and different. Learning to look at paintings can open your eyes to a new way of seeing.

Where to Look

Of all the pictures you have ever seen, which do you like best? Maybe it is a poster on your wall, or a postcard, or an illustration in a book. If you are lucky enough to live near a gallery or a museum, perhaps it is a famous original painting. Have you ever looked really closely at that favorite picture, or thought about how or when it was made?

How to see

Usually, when people look at a picture, their eyes scan it to get a vague idea of what is going on.

Maybe at first glance, you start by loving the colors, or the shapes, or the special feelings a picture stirs up in you. That is a good way to begin. But, if you look really closely at pictures and learn something about how they are painted, the pictures will "speak" to you.

Have a look at *A Winter Scene with Skaters* on pages 6–7. At first, you notice lots of people skating, a big building, and a lovely tree. Now have a closer look. Does the picture suggest noises to you? Perhaps the sound of ice cracking, or children laughing, or skates going swish-swish across the ice? Can you hear a horse's hooves clopping over the ice, or the hum of excited conversation? See how your imagination begins to work when you give the painting a chance to speak?

Make a view finder

Sometimes, there is so much to look at in a picture that you want to concentrate on a bit at a time. A little bit of a picture is called a detail. Use a view finder to study details.
1. On a piece of thin cardboard 4 in. square, measure and mark 1 in. in from the edge. Pencil a line through all the marks.
2. Then draw a colored line as shown. Cut along the color to make two L-shaped hooks.
3. Move your hooks around to make the view finder bigger, smaller, or a different shape. Use them to look closely at real pictures in a gallery or at reproductions in a book.

The original painting is the one created by the artist. It is often very valuable because it is the only one in the world.

In the art gallery or museum, where the original usually hangs, someone takes a photograph of the painting.

The photographic film is used to make hundreds and hundreds of prints or reproductions of the original painting.

The original painting can be reproduced in books or as postcards and posters which you can put on the wall.

How big is the original?

The prints you see in books or on postcards are often much smaller than the original painting. When you go to a gallery or a museum, there will be lots of surprises!

Some of the original paintings printed in this book might take up a whole wall of your bedroom or even the classroom wall at school. For instance, the picture on pages 14–15 of the people swimming and sunbathing looks small enough to cover up with your hands. But the real painting is huge – 6 by 9 feet. In this book, in fact, only the round skating picture on pages 6–7 and the Persian picture on page 9 are about the same size as the original paintings. At a museum, you might see paintings of every size, from huge portraits to tiny miniatures.

Captions to help

The caption for each picture in the book tells you how big the original painting is. It also gives you the picture's title, the date it was painted, and the name of the painter.

If you look carefully at the pictures themselves, you might find the painter's signature. In the front of the skating picture on pages 6–7, you will see the letters H.A., standing for Hendrick Avercamp. They have been worked into a neat little design called a monogram.

Skating in the Frosty Air

There is so much happening in this little picture of a winter scene: people skating, people falling over, people pushing carts, sitting around, or just looking! The Dutch artist who painted it made the picture look crowded and busy. In fact the painter, called Hendrick Avercamp, could not talk. This might explain why he liked to share all the things he noticed. He could then say, "Look at that" in pictures instead of words.

What is everybody doing?

Can you see a boy throwing snowballs at a girl or a horse-drawn sleigh moving across the ice? Do you see a man tying a woman's skate for her? If you look very closely, you'll see someone at a window and three other people sitting on a boat.

Far, far away

The painting is only 16 in. in diameter – a little larger than you see it here – and yet everything is so clear that you can spot things even in the distance. It is like gazing through a telescope. Look, there is a church a long way off, and people seem to be walking for miles across the ice. To get this deep, distant look, Hendrick Avercamp painted big people and trees in the front of the picture and made everything else look smaller. Measure the tree halfway back on the right-hand side, and compare it with the tree at the front. You will see that it is only one-third the size. The proper word for showing distance in a painting is perspective.

Look again

Did you notice the man crouched by the tree, right at the front of the picture? The front of a painting is called the foreground. And can you see a group of grand people dancing? They are in the middle ground of the picture. Then, there's a castle, and further off, the church, more people, and another sleigh. These smaller things are in the background of the picture.

Bring the people to life

Can you make up an imaginary story about some of the skaters in the middle ground? Which people do you think live in the castle, and which live in town?

background

middle ground

foreground

A Winter Scene with Skaters
by Hendrick Avercamp
painted about 1609
size: 1 ft. 4 in. diameter

7

The Story of a Deadly Rose

Here is a mysterious picture. A king sits on a throne with his nobles around him. On the floor, a man lies dead. See how his turban has fallen off? There is a rose near his body. Another man looks on with a wicked grin – he might even be clapping his hands in glee. All the other people look amazed.

Yet, you cannot tell the whole truth just by looking at the picture, however hard you try. That is because this picture is an illustration for a book. It was painted over four hundred years ago in Persia. (Persia is now called Iran.) The picture makes much more sense when you know the story that goes with it – and here is the story of a deadly rose.

Once upon a time ...
Hundreds of years ago, when Persian Sultans ruled huge empires, two doctors had a contest to become the king's favorite. The first doctor – or physician, as they are sometimes called – made a deadly pill from a long list of secret ingredients. It caused fearful stomachaches and convulsions which killed people. This doctor dared his rival to take the pill. The second physician swallowed it with a smile. He had already taken a magic pill of his own, and the deadly medicine had no effect at all.

The Sultan and his court watched eagerly as the second physician plucked a beautiful red rose from the garden. He kissed the petals, whispered a spell into the heart of the flower, and offered it to his enemy. When the first doctor raised it to his lips, he immediately fell down dead. His cunning rival had won.

What the Sultan saw
This is the scene the Persian artist, Aqa Mirak, chose to illustrate in the storybook. He wanted to please his Sultan, Shah Tahmasp of Tabriz, so he painted the Sultan of the story to look like the Shah himself. You can see him sitting on his throne under a canopy.

In Persia, people used to sit on pillows instead of chairs. They put their books on a stand made of carved wood. The artist wanted Shah Tahmasp to enjoy looking at ducks in the pond, the beautiful tiles on the floor, the flowers in the garden, and a traveler's horse in the distance. You could not see all these details at once if you stood in one place and looked at the scene. But then, Aqa Mirak did not worry very much about perspective: he was more interested in getting all these things into his picture. Imagine the Shah turning the pages of the small, leather-bound book decorated with gold. He would probably smile with pleasure at the beauty of *The Physicians' Duel*.

Colors like jewels
The colors are beautiful. It is like looking into a little jewelry box. The colors really glow because they were made from precious stones and costly metals. The green of the Sultan's tunic may be made from a stone called malachite, crushed to a powder and mixed with gum to make a paint. Real silver and gold were beaten into a thin film and added to the painting. All these rich materials made the book a worthy gift for the Shah.

**The Physicians' Duel
by Aqa Mirak
probably painted
between 1539–1543
size: 11½ in. × 8 in.**

8

War and Pain

This picture shows you the pain and suffering of war. A woman screams in agony, her dead child in her arms. A horse rears in torment, a spear through its body. A man lies dying, his broken sword in hand. On the right, a woman with her clothes on fire falls from a burning house. Everything looks ugly and distorted.

A town called Guernica

The picture was painted by Pablo Picasso in 1937. The painter was extremely angry about the civil war that was tearing apart his country, Spain. He was especially horrified by the news of a savage and senseless bombing attack by airplanes on a little town called Guernica (pronounced *Gernicka*).

Picasso painted this picture to show how ugly war is and how it damages and destroys – and he named the picture after the town. *Guernica* is a huge picture – the painting is bigger than the wall of an ordinary living room.

Listen to the sounds

There are no colors in this picture: only blacks, whites, and grays. Maybe the painter felt that colors are too beautiful for such a serious subject. Take a close look at the picture and let it speak to you. You can almost feel the confusion and terror. Can you hear some of the dreadful noises – the screams, shouts, and groans? You can see that most of the people and animals have their mouths open as if they are screaming in pain. The artist also made everything look broken, crooked, and ugly. What sounds and feelings do the crisscross lines and shapes suggest to you?

The painter's mood

Perhaps the two strongest feelings expressed by *Guernica* are "I am angry" and "I am hurt." How has the artist passed on his mood to you? You have heard the awful sounds, and noticed the sharp outlines and lack of color. Now, look at the faces. They are just big white shapes with staring eyes and yelling mouths. You can see two eyes in every head, no matter which way it is facing. Like a dead person's stare, the eyes are open and fixed in terror.

At the top of the picture dangles an unshaded electric light-bulb. This glaring light reaches out to reveal the horrors of war. The rays of light from the bulb are like sharp, jagged teeth. The painter made them spiky to set our nerves on edge.

All these details helped Picasso tell you that a terrible thing was happening in this town.

Speaking to everyone
Have you ever seen a news report
of a war going on? Have you
thought about how people and
animals are hurt in wars?
Although Picasso made his
picture because of what was
happening in Spain, *Guernica*
could be a picture protesting
about all wars. That is one reason
it has become famous – people all
over the world can look at it and
understand what it is saying.

Guernica
by Pablo Picasso
painted 1937
size: 12 ft. × 25 ft. 6 in.

A Double Celebration

This painting by Carlo Crivelli looks complicated at first glance. That is because the artist put two special stories together to make one special picture.

The Annunciation
The first is the story of the Annunciation, which comes from the Bible. "Annunciation" is just another word for "news" or "announcement." It is about the Angel Gabriel's visit to the Virgin Mary to tell her that she had been chosen by God to give birth to His son, Jesus. There is the angel kneeling in the street. And there is Mary, inside the house, with her head bowed in prayer.

But the scene does not look at all like Palestine, the Middle Eastern country in which Mary lived. Instead of hot, dusty streets, there are cool stone courtyards and potted plants. You can guess from the fine clothes and richly decorated buildings that the scene is set in some other time and place. And that brings us to the second story!

In 1482, the little Italian town of Ascoli was given certain rights of self-government by the Pope. The people of Ascoli first heard the news on March 25th – the day when people celebrate the Angel's visit to Mary.

See how cleverly the artist linked the story of the Annunciation with the news about Ascoli's independence? He painted the Angel Gabriel kneeling before Mary's house with Saint Emidius, the patron saint (or special protector), of the town. The Saint holds in his hands a model of Ascoli. He is showing it to Gabriel as if to say "Look at our town. We are so proud of it!"

A town within a town
The model of Ascoli shows that it was a strongly fortified town. Look at the defense tower and the sturdy gateway set into the protective wall.

Crivelli also put a lot of other details into this tiny part of his picture. There are windows, doorways, and arches. You can even see the lines in the brickwork and the patterns on the roofs.

Learning about the past
Carlo Crivelli's painting looks old and historical now, but it tells us something about Italy in his own time – the 15th century. The citizens who have come out to hear the news are wearing their ordinary clothes. The Virgin Mary looks like a noble lady of the town with her pretty dress and luxurious house. This picture tells us what the clothes, the furniture, and the houses were like. Since photography was not invented until about 100 years ago, pictures like this reveal a lot about the past.

Detailed designs
Crivelli must have loved making patterns. You notice the buildings and the lovely designs almost before you notice the people in the picture. Look at the carved patterns on the pillars of Mary's house. There are more running around the second-floor balcony. Then, there are patterned ceilings, carpets, clothes, and a curtain. Even the arched bridge is decorated with elaborate designs.

Count the patterns
How many different patterns are there? Do not forget to count the peacock's tail!

The Annunciation with Saint Emidius by Carlo Crivelli painted 1486 size: 6 ft. × 4 ft. 6 in.

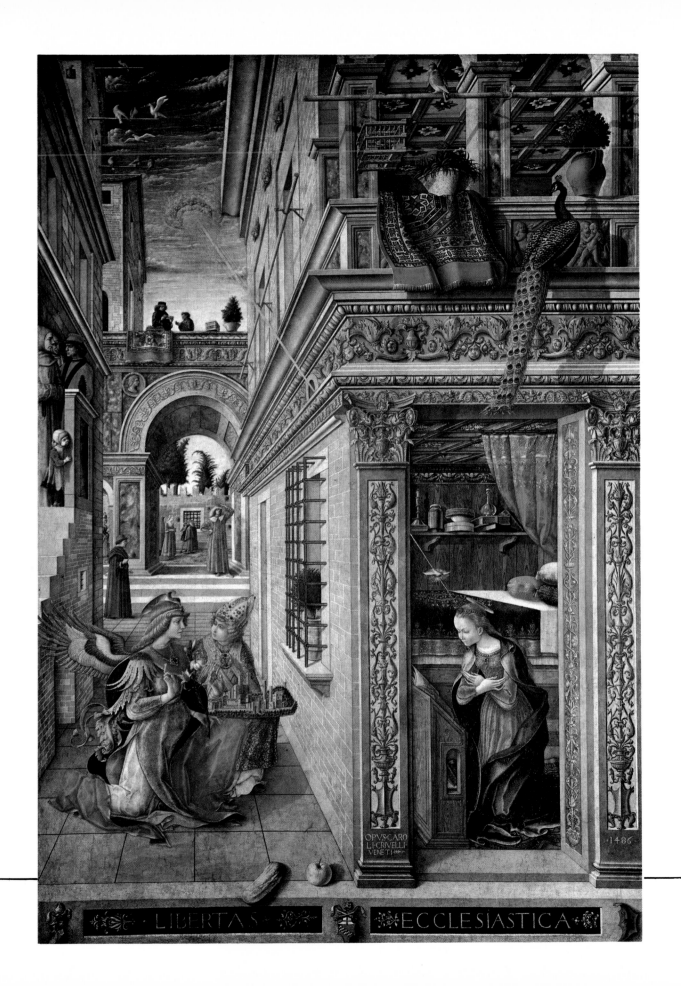

A Lazy Summer's Day

Can you imagine how hot the hottest summer day can be? If you look at this picture, you can almost feel that kind of heat. This painting shows some people lazing away a hot afternoon. A few are resting, sunbathing, or swimming, and others are yachting and rowing. The boy in the orange hat could be whistling or calling to a friend. But all this activity is very slow. You cannot see any details in the faces or the clothing of the figures on the river bank. They look lazy and still – they might even be dozing off in the sun.

There are no clear details in the scenery, either. Everything looks hazy. But notice how the sunlight dances on the trees and how it makes the water shimmer in a thousand places. And can you see the smoke floating up into the sky from those distant chimneys? There is hardly a breath of wind. The artist painted a picture of stillness and peace.

The bold young artist
The French artist, Georges Seurat, painted the *Bathers at Asnières* when he was twenty-four years old. At that time, most big paintings were of gods and goddesses or of great scenes from history. But Seurat did something unusual: he painted a very large picture of ordinary people enjoying themselves. (The figures in the painting are the same size as real people.)

Arranging the people
To get the feeling of a sunny atmosphere, Seurat stood on the river bank at Asnières (a suburb of Paris) to sketch the colors of the scene. Back in his studio, he made black crayon drawings of people.

When he began to paint the picture, Seurat treated it a bit like a huge stage set. He painted the scenery; then he arranged the figures in it.

New ways with color
Seurat tried to paint colors exactly like the ones that he noticed when he stood on the river bank at Asnières. Look closely at the picture, and you will find that he used crisscross strokes in various colors for the grass. He painted smooth, thick lines of color for the water. Both the grass and the water seem to reflect warm yellow sunlight.

But Seurat also experimented with combinations of color. The boy's orange hat is made up of tiny dots of different colors crowded together.

Later on, Seurat painted all his pictures by making forms and shapes out of thousands of little colored dots of paint. When the painting is seen from a distance, the dots of brilliant color merge together to suggest other colors. This way of painting became known as pointillism.

Experiment with dots
If you have lots of patience, you could try painting a little dot picture of a hat. Put yellow and blue dots very close together so that they merge into green.

**Bathers at Asnières
by Georges Seurat
painted 1883–1884
size: 6 ft. × 9 ft.**

Look carefully at the boy's hat. It is not like the rest of the picture. See how dots of color merge together into orange? Seurat repainted the hat this way a long time after he had actually finished the picture.

Sinbad Goes To Sea

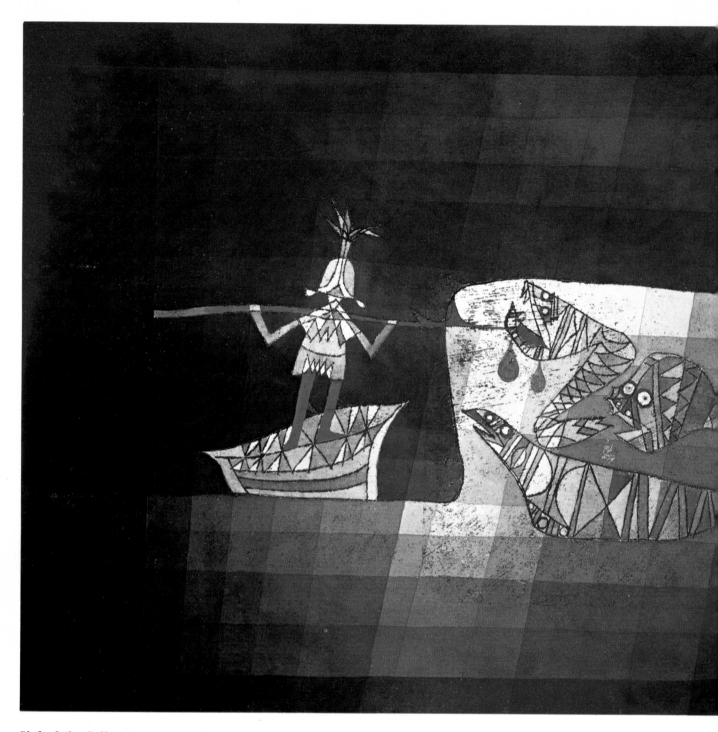

Sinbad the Sailor
by Paul Klee
painted 1923
size: 1 ft. 3 in. × 1 ft. 8 in.

Here is a painting of a little stick-fisherman and three very large fish. Do you think it is amusing that the fish look big enough to swallow both the man and his boat? And the fisherman is a rather strange character. Look at those spiky feathers on his head and the zigzag patterns on his clothes. The boat, too, is much smaller than any ordinary fishing boat. Look how the man, his boat, and the fish are all placed in an ocean of colored squares. No ocean really looks like this. In fact, nothing in the picture looks realistic.

Can you imagine why Paul Klee (pronounced *Clay*) chose to paint his picture this way?

A magical tale

Sinbad the Sailor is a mythical person, and the stories about him are full of magic. In Klee's picture, you can tell that Sinbad is harpooning a fish, but neither the man nor the fish looks real. That is because the artist was painting a fable – a kind of fairy tale – and not a real scene.

Was the painter having fun?

Look at the three fish. Although each one is different, the patterns of their scales match each other. And what about the pattern on Sinbad's shirt – it matches the pattern on his boat. Have you ever heard of a sailor who painted his boat to match his clothes?

Perhaps Klee was simply having fun making colorful designs and shapes.

Panels of color

Notice how the sea changes color as your eyes move from one square to another. Klee carefully graded his colors from deep blues and browns at the edges to light blues and white at the center. In this way, he suggests the rise and fall of the ocean, and how its color changes all the time.

Follow the lines of the squares to see how they join up with the patterns on Sinbad, his boat, and the fish. It looks as if the artist played a game with his colored checks.

The thoughtful artist

Klee's painting certainly does not look solemn, does it? The artist enjoyed making his colorful patterns. But he also thought seriously about man and nature. Klee believed that all living creatures exist together in balanced harmony. That helps to explain why he built everything in his picture into one harmonious pattern.

Trace the lines

Put a sheet of tracing paper over one of the fish, and then trace all the lines that make up its body. You will see that Klee's patterns are like tiny fish bones.

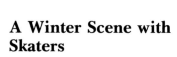

Now What Would You Say?

Here you see the sizes of the pictures compared with the children looking at them. Would you agree with any of these comments about the pictures?

Guernica

"It looks like a puzzle."

"It is spooky."

"The horse looks like newspaper writing."

"He must have been really angry to paint a picture that big."

"I understand what he is saying, but it still looks silly."

"That is the picture that will make me go away and think."

"It looks like it is from a comic book."

The Annunciation

"The lady must be holy – she has got a plate on her head."

"I would feel like a stranger in that scene."

"Everything looks rich."

"It looks like a picture from another country."

"Look at the size of that peanut!"

The Physicians' Duel

"I thought a 'duel' meant with swords. Poison is different."

"It is beautiful. I love the detail and color."

"It looks flat. The people are standing on each other's heads."

"It is like a cartoon because it is telling a story."

A Winter Scene with Skaters

"I love it because skating is fun and I can imagine it."

"It is like looking at a scene through a small hole."

"The tree is haunted and misty."

"I like the way the view gets smaller as it goes away."

"The poor man in the front looks cold – he is hunched up."

Bathers at Asnières

"It looks as though he has put the color on with a knife."

"It makes me want to go swimming."

"It is boring because the people look so posed."

Sinbad the Sailor

"It is an imaginary land – you do not have zigzag fish."

"The painter had a bad dream."

"It looks like it is in a movie because the edges are dark.

Everybody is Different

If you half-close your eyes and look at this picture, a wonderful thing happens: it glows with light and movement. See the way the grass seems to shine and change color as the breeze blows across it?

The artist, Claude Monet (pronounced *Mon-nay*), was fascinated by the way light falls on plants and water. He wanted to tell you how a lily pond looks on a warm day.

Monet did not show you any precise details. You cannot see the leaves of the grass, the petals of the flowers, or the branches of the trees. But you can really feel how lush and strong the grass grows around the water's edge, and how the light dances across the pond.

Light and color

The Water-Lily Pond is a picture of Monet's own garden which he planned and built himself. The artist stood in the garden and painted the colors of the lily pond just as he saw them. In his painting, he tried to capture his first impression of the scene.

You cannot find any black in the picture, can you? All the shadows are made up of blues, greens, and other dark colors. Monet enjoyed piling rich colors into his painting. See how his brushmarks of color mingle to give you a vivid impression of light falling on the scene?

**The Water-Lily Pond
by Claude Monet
painted about 1899
size: 2 ft. 11 in. × 3 ft.**

A garden of patterns

Look at the trees and flowers in *The Physicians' Duel.* You can see every detail, but the garden looks unreal compared with Monet's. You cannot feel the movement and see the light bathing the scene. That is because Aqa Mirak loved making designs on all the surfaces of his picture. He was not interested in showing light and movement.

The delicate wooden bridge

Now look closely at Monet's bridge. The bridge is a sign that people do go into the garden, even though we see nobody in the picture. But it is a flimsy-looking bridge. You cannot see any supports. And you cannot see where the bridge begins and ends. It seems to float above the water just as the lilies are floating on the pond. Monet was not concerned with showing the construction of the bridge – it is the play of light and shadow on it that really caught his interest.

A bridge of solid stone

Remember the bridge Crivelli painted in his picture, *The Annunciation*? It is not at all like Monet's bridge, is it? Look at the solid, powerful arch – you can tell that it would easily bear the people walking on it. Crivelli liked the architecture of the bridge. He explained every part of its construction – the supports, the arch, even the decorations.

See for yourself

Do you begin to see that artists choose to paint in different ways? That is one of the reasons why looking at pictures is so exciting: painters show us all kinds of ways to look at the world we live in.

Find out how differently we all see things by playing a game with friends. Someone says, for instance, "railroad station." Each player scribbles down the first words that come to mind. They might be as different as "noisy," "steamy," "heavy suitcases," "shiny engines." Try the game with other words such as "school" or "football field." Soon you will find that everyone has his own special way of seeing.

Looking at Nature

Here is a beautiful painting of a vase of flowers by the Dutch artist Jan van Huijsum (pronounced *How-zum*). Not many people could draw a picture as precisely as this! You can see every leaf and petal – even the spots on the eggs in the little nest. But the painting is not true to nature: you would never see all these flowers blooming at the same time.

Flowers in still life
It did not matter to Huijsum that his picture is not true to a season. He wanted to say, "Look at all the marvelous natural things we can enjoy!" Except he did not use words to say this – he painted a picture of all the lovely flowers he could find. This painting is a still life – that is, a picture of deliberately arranged things.

A bee's eye view
When you look at a piece of moss or a flower through a magnifying glass, you discover a whole new world of intricate details and patterns. But what would you do if someone asked you to draw that flower? Would you put in everything you *know* is there, or would you only show what you can see with your naked eye?

**Flowers in a Terracotta Vase
by Jan van Huijsum
painted 1736–1737
size: 4 ft. 6 in. × 3 ft.**

Movement in a pond

What was Monet trying to say about the flowers in his lily pond? It is clear that he was painting a natural scene and not a still life. Monet did not show us any details in the lilies. We do not see all the petals and leaves the artist *knew* were there. Instead, we get an impression of dappled light falling on the flowers and their lazy movement as the pond ripples in the breeze. Monet was also interested in paint itself – its texture and variety of colors. How many different colors can you see in this patch of lilies?

Both Monet's and Huijsum's paintings are about nature. But each artist makes us see and feel something different. All good paintings affect us this way. They are a bit like music – we can sense what is going on without having to think it out.

All kinds of trees

Sometimes, a painter uses plants or trees to help set a scene or mood in a picture.

Look at the tree from Hendrick Avercamp's picture, *A Winter Scene with Skaters*. Its sharp outline tells us that the air is crisp and cold. The painting is really about skaters, but this bare tree helped the artist show the winter cold.

Below are some trees from Seurat's picture, *Bathers at Asnières*. See how the hazy sunlight shines on them? This tiny part of the picture adds to the feeling that it is a hot, still day on the river bank.

A little potted plant

You probably remember that the picture, *The Annunciation*, has people and buildings in it. But did you notice this potted plant on the balcony of Mary's house? The leaves are drawn very precisely and clearly. And the pot is a lovely shape. Crivelli put this little still-life detail into his painting to make Mary's house look real and lived-in.

Find the details

There are other still-life details in Crivelli's picture, including more potted plants, a piece of fruit, and a vegetable. Look back to *The Annunciation* on page 13, and see if you can find them all.

Remember that you can look closely at a tiny part of the painting if you make two cardboard hooks as shown on pages 4–5. You could try using them to look at the still-life details in Crivelli's picture. (Did you also notice books, dishes, a wooden birdcage, and a candle? These are still-life details, too.)

All Kinds of Horses

Here is some action! Look how the hooves slip as the horse scrambles around the bare, dusty hill. This muscular animal and the equally tough cowboy work together, leaning into the hillside to keep their balance. See how Frederic Remington painted the mane and tail in rough brushstrokes? This gives the impression that the horse is really moving. The horse and rider look important – and lonely, too – because the background is painted with so little detail.

Today, cowboys and cowgirls drive cattle across tame land. But, when Remington painted this picture, the Wild West still existed.

Nobleman's steed

The Persian horse and its rider (below) look very elegant. There is something about the curve of the horse's neck that suggests it is a noble animal.

This horse is part of the storybook illustration, *The Physicians' Duel*. But it does not seem "alive." The artist is more interested in the patterns and shape of the horse than in making you feel that it is real.

**The Cowboy
by Frederic Remington
painted 1902
size: 3 ft. 4 in. × 2ft. 4 in.**

A horse in pain

This animal is all twisted and peculiar, not at all like horses look in real life. Yet, you can definitely tell it is a horse – look at the outstretched neck and the bared teeth. You can hear the horse neighing very loudly in pain and fright.

Remember this horse from the picture, *Guernica*? The artist, Picasso, could have drawn it accurately if he wanted to. But he twisted the shape of the horse on purpose to make us feel the pain and ugliness of the scene.

**A Horse Frightened
by Lightning
by Théodore Géricault
painted about 1820
size: 1 ft. 7 in. × 2 ft.**

Look at the picture of a proud race horse by Géricault. How beautiful he is! He looks fit and excited: his coat is shiny, and every nerve in his body is tense with anticipation. It is not just the way the artist has drawn the horse's body and legs that makes the animal look so alert. There is more to it than that. A painter can exaggerate details to make a picture more exciting. This horse looks nervous – you can see the whites of his eyes. The painter

also put in rumbling black clouds and a heavy sky for dramatic effect.

These details add excitement and tension. They make the horse seem more alive, more swift, and energetic. In fact, although the horse is standing still, this picture seems to say, "Look how fast and powerful the horse is!"

Look at other animals

Have you got a cat or a dog? Or does a friend have one that you could look at? If you wanted to tell people about it by painting its picture, what would you show? The leathery pads on its feet? The alertness of its ears? Perhaps the joyful wag of its tail? Or the glossy coat and bright eyes of a very healthy animal?

How Painters See People

Without using words, we tell each other lots of things. Your mother knows you are not feeling well, for instance, if you look "a bit pale." And what does blushing tell people?

The look, or "expression," on your face gives out an even clearer message. Add a gesture to a facial expression, and your message is clearest of all. What does a clenched fist say? Artists have always known that the most expressive parts of the body are the face and hands. Look below at the cartoon character. The artist, Patrick Hughes, made the cartoon figure look stupid by putting its eyes close together and by cutting off its head below the brain. And the gesture is unmistakable – he is sneering rudely at something.

This drawing is on the cover of a catalog of modern paintings, and the caption with it says, "A child of six could do it!" What do you think Patrick Hughes meant?

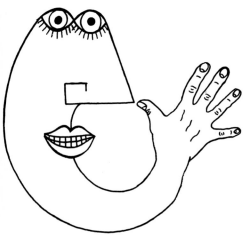

What is a portrait?
A painting which mainly shows a person's face is called a portrait. When you look at portraits made hundreds of years ago, you soon realize that people do not change much through the ages. Their dress is usually different, but their features or expressions often seem familiar.

**Portrait of a Man in Blue
by Titian
painted sometime
between 1511–1576
size: 1 ft. 7 in. × 2 ft. 2 in.**

Look at the man in blue shown here. His portrait was painted by an Italian artist named Titian (pronounced *Tish-un*) over 400 years ago. But you might see someone in the street today with a face – even a hairstyle and a beard – just like his.

The man has a mysterious, half-smile on his face. Is he pleased to have his portrait painted? Does he look vain, as if he is saying, "Well, I *am* a handsome fellow, and now the world will know it?" Or does his expression tell you something else? Notice how his eyes seem to follow you wherever you go.

One kind of perfection
Have another look at *The Annunciation* – the picture with the Virgin Mary in it – on page 13. Can you see how the painter made her face look delicate by painting fine lines for her eyes and mouth? Her expression is serene. She looks lovely. But her features are too perfect for you to feel that you would ever see a face like hers in the street! Crivelli painted her this way to show that she is holy and special.

Sitting in the sun
Compare the portrait of the man in blue with this boy's face from Seurat's painting, *Bathers at Asnières*. The man looks likes a real person. The boy, however, does not seem to have a personality at all. His face has no expression – you cannot even see his eyes or mouth. But you get the impression that the boy is feeling lazy and hot. See the reddish-blue tinge on his face? It looks very much like the color skin gets in hot sunlight.

A face in torment
Here is one of those strange, frightened faces from the Picasso picture, *Guernica*. The woman's head is ugly. Her gaping mouth and outstretched neck show you the agony she feels because her child is dead. The face is disturbing partly because the eyes are so crooked and the mouth is much bigger than normal. Pablo Picasso exaggerated the woman's features on purpose to show how horrible war is.

Add some modern clothes
Collect pictures of historical people, and see which ones look modern. An easy way to do this is to give the faces up-to-date clothes.

Cut a hole in a sheet of paper big enough to put the picture of the person's face underneath. Then, draw a body wearing jeans and a T-shirt or a dress. The result is sometimes very funny and surprising!

What Clothes Tell You

One of the things you notice when you look at pictures is how artists paint in different ways. But, you can also look at pictures as though they are "photographs of the past." You can discover how people lived in other centuries and other countries by studying the details of their clothes, the insides of their houses, the streets, and so on.

How do you dress?

At school, you wear everyday clothes. Maybe you wear the clothes you like best of all when you go out. There are different clothes for different occasions. What you wear says something about you; *how* you wear your clothes tells even more.

Wealth and power

An artist knows that the way people dress can give us clues about who they are, how they live, and what they are like. Look at the portrait of Queen Elizabeth I of England. There is no mistaking the wealth and power of this grand lady. See the precious stones set into the band that runs down the front of her dress? Can you find a heart-shaped, jeweled pendant on the band? And look at all the fine lace embroidered with gold streaming out behind the Queen's head. Even the handle of the luxurious feather fan she holds is covered in jewels.

This colorful painting shows us how a rich and royal person dressed in the 16th century. But history tells us that, while Queen Elizabeth dressed in velvet and gold, the people of her kingdom wore rough wool tunics and plain cotton smocks.

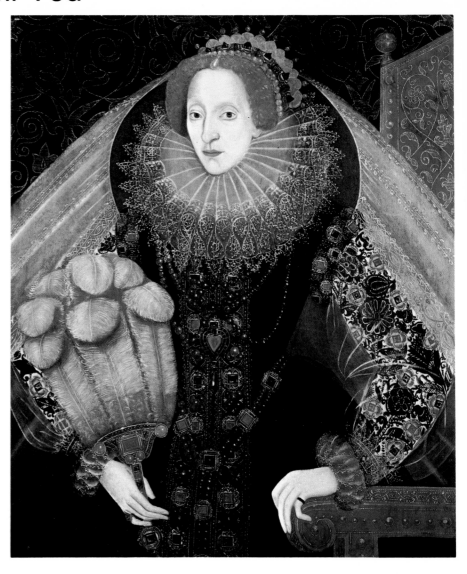

Queen Elizabeth I
painter unknown
painted about 1585
size: 3 ft. 1 in. × 2 ft. 8 in.

500 years ago

Here is the little girl peeping around the wall from the picture, *The Annunciation*. What can you tell about her? She is clearly not poor and hungry – look at those plump cheeks! She is very neatly dressed, with a tight cap over her head and what look like pearls sewn around the edge of her pinafore. Perhaps she is the daughter of a rich merchant or storekeeper. And what is she dressed for? Maybe she is waiting for school to begin, or for her parents to take her to visit relatives.

These are questions which people who study history through pictures try to answer. Learning about the past is much more interesting when you know how people dressed.

Merchants and peasants

You can see in *A Winter Scene with Skaters* that people dressed in different ways at that time. Two of the skaters are very richly dressed and obviously have lots of money. The other two people look very plain and simple, and perhaps are farming folk from a village nearby. Now look closely at the details. Do we use skates like these? And the hats – can you see that two are round and that one has feathers?

Luxury in Persia

Sometimes, of course, it is hard to tell if the painter is being truthful or just imagining fancy clothes. In the Persian picture, *The Physicians' Duel*, every noble has gold decoration on his clothes. Do you think everyone could afford such costly embroidery, or was the artist just making his picture look pretty and decorative by putting patterns on all the colorful tunics?

Make a scrapbook

Even the smallest detail in a painting can be interesting. You could spend hours in a gallery or a library just looking at such details as shoes, hats, and hairstyles.

Why not start a postcard scrapbook of different clothing? You could choose pictures showing the dress of a particular century or country. Or collect pictures of people in ruffs – the kind of stiff white collar the Queen is wearing. That would be unusual. While you are looking, see if you can find any pictures of historical clothing that is fashionable today.

How Sharp are Your Eyes?

Now here is a chance to see what you have noticed in each of the pictures shown on pages 6–17 of this book. Here are the names of the six pictures again.

1. *A Winter Scene with Skaters*
2. *The Physicians' Duel*
3. *Guernica*
4. *The Annunciation*
5. *Bathers at Asnières*
6. *Sinbad the Sailor*

Can you guess which painting each of the details comes from? Before you turn any pages, or look at the answers on page 46, here are a few clues.

Let us take the first detail, which shows the little boat. One of the big pictures in this book is painted in blacks, whites, and grays with strong, hard lines. That was *Guernica* by Picasso. But this boat is softly colored, so it is not from that.

There is a boat in the painting *Sinbad the Sailor* by Klee. Did you notice how it is made up of neat, flat, and distinctly colored shapes? The boat in the detail looks rounded, though, and has dark shadows painted on it, so it is not from that one either!

What about the picture of the Virgin Mary and the Angel? It is very carefully and precisely drawn, with lots of details in the buildings and clothes. So it cannot be from that one! Now you only have a few pictures left to think about. Which one shares the same color and mood as the boat?

a

b

c

d

e

f

The painter's handwriting

All those differences you noticed are part of what is called a painter's style. Every artist paints pictures in a very special and individual way. It is just like handwriting. Perhaps you can recognize the writing of your best friend, your mother, or your teacher. Style is just another way of saying that an artist has a special kind of "handwriting" when painting.

From Cave Wall to Canvas

When you decide to paint a picture, you probably go into a store and buy a box of water colors, or maybe even some tubes of oil paint. That is the easy part! But have you ever wondered what colors come from, or how paints are made?

Nature's wealth of color

Most colors are made from things in the natural world: earth, rocks, plants, precious stones and metals – even the dried bodies of insects.

To make colors, the raw material must first be ground into a powder called a pigment. Then the pigment is mixed with a medium to make it liquid and a binder to make it sticky. Water is a medium; oil (from seeds and flowers) is another. Gum (from trees and plants), glue, and eggs are binders.

Remember the blue of the grinning doctor's robe in the Persian picture on page 9? It was probably made from a precious stone called lapis lazuli, crushed into a powder and mixed with gum to make a paint. A green pigment is ground from *terre verte* ("green earth"), and a strong yellow comes from yellow ocher, a kind of clay. Raw sienna – an earth found at Siena in Italy – makes a clear, delicate yellow. A lovely rose-colored pigment

comes from the powdered root of the rose madder plant. Scarlet is made from ground-up female cochineal beetles.

The world's first artists

Above is a picture of a prehistoric bison painted with colors made from natural things. It was put on a cave wall at Altamira in Spain, about 20,000 years ago. To make pictures like this, primitive artists

first scratched an outline with a piece of flint, and then filled in the color. They made brown, yellow, and reddish pigments by grinding up iron ores with rocks. They mixed their pigments with plant juices or animal blood or fat to make them into paint. Black paint was made from soot or

The delicate touch

Look below at the Japanese picture of a kingfisher. See how transparent the paint looks? The paper almost seems to shine through those delicate blues and browns. That is because the artist has painted with water color – a soft, washy kind of paint. Water colors are made by mixing pigments with gum or water itself.

Yamanaka Shönen used only a few brushstrokes to describe the kingfisher, yet it is very realistic and beautiful.

water color

gouache color

oil color

charcoal, and white from chalk.

The artists put paint on with their fingers, or with brushes made from fur, feathers, or chewed-up twigs.

Can you imagine how much time and hard work it took to make a picture this way?

Later on, artists began to paint on house walls, panels of wood, sheets of paper, or very thin leather. Then, in the 15th century, artists began to paint on canvas. This is specially-treated cloth, usually linen or cotton, stretched tightly over a wooden frame to hold it in place.

Kingfisher
by Yamanaka Shönen
painted sometime
between 1806–1820
size: 10½ in. × 7½ in.

Paints for every purpose

Today, all kinds of paints come ready-made in tubes, and each type has different qualities. Water color looks soft and transparent when used. It is quite different from poster color, which gives a flat, matt finish. Gouache (pronounced *goo-ash*) and tempera are opaque paints similar to poster colors. All these paints are used on paper.

Oil paint is thick and shiny, and is used to paint on canvas, wood, or special paper. Most pictures in this book were painted with oils. Because oil paint takes a long time to dry (between eight hours and two days!), many modern artists use quick-drying acrylic paints instead. They have the same glossy quality as oils.

Make your own paint

You will need a stick of white or colored chalk, two teaspoons of vegetable oil, a chopping board, and a metal spoon. (Ask before you use these things.) Break the chalk up, then grind it into a very fine powder with the back of the spoon. Add the oil, drop by drop, stirring the mixture until it is smooth.

A Thousand and One Colors

What is your favorite color? Red, yellow, green, or something else? Think about it for a moment, and then try to imagine how you would describe that color in words. It does not help much to say, for instance, "I like green." One person might think of "grass green" and another might think of "bottle green." There are so many different shades of colors – and each one affects people in different ways.

Blue, blue, or blue?

Think about the word "blue." List some different blues you have seen: sky blue, ink blue, and perhaps cornflower blue. Now look for blue things around your home, and try to think of the special word that tells you exactly how each one looks. How would you describe the blue of the man's sleeve on page 26 of this book? Smoky blue? Hyacinth blue? Sea blue?

If none of these fits, perhaps in the future you will think of that particular shade of blue as "Titian sleeve" blue!

Playing with colors

You and your friends can play the word game with other colors: think of "toast brown" instead of plain brown; or "a thundercloud gray" instead of ordinary gray. Each player scores one point for every new descriptive word.

Mixing basic colors

Red, yellow, and blue are called primary colors. If you mix them in the combinations shown above, you will make three secondary colors – orange, green, and purple.

There are many kinds of red, yellow, and blue. Try to find colors like the ones shown. The red is called magenta – it looks pink, but it is the best red to use for mixing.

Experiment

Put a scrap of red paper on white paper; then look at the red paper on brown. Which makes the red more vivid? Now try putting red on its opposite color, green. See how different combinations affect your eyes? Colors look stronger when their opposites are present. So blue looks bluer when it is near orange; and yellow is stronger if it is near purple.

Making shades of color

If you mix different amounts of primary colors, you will get varying shades of secondaries. Get a magnifying glass and look at the secondary colors above. See how purple is made up of dots of blue and magenta red? Green has blue and yellow dots; orange has red and yellow ones. Browns are mixtures of all three colors.

Match the colors

Look carefully at the paints on these six palettes. Now think back to the six pictures shown on pages 6–17 of this book.

1. *A Winter Scene with Skaters*
2. *The Physicians' Duel*
3. *Guernica*
4. *The Annunciation*
5. *Bathers at Asnières*
6. *Sinbad the Sailor*

One palette matches the colors of one of these six pictures. Can you put the right letter with the right number?

(Palette d has only black, white, and gray on it, so you should be able to match that one! The answers are on page 46.)

a   b   c   d

Opposite colors

The colors opposite each other in the center of this wheel are called opposite colors: green and red; orange and blue; yellow and purple. (They are sometimes called complementary colors.)

The outer circle of the wheel shows just a few of the many shades of color you can make by mixing different amounts of primary colors together.

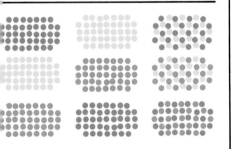

A dotty idea

Remember how Seurat crowded little dots of paint together? And you have seen how dots make up secondary colors printed on this page. Try it yourself by making lots of magenta red and yellow dots; blue and yellow dots; blue and red dots. Stand four yards away and see what happens. You should be able to see orange, green, and purple.

The Snail
by Henri Matisse
painted 1953
size: 9 ft. square

Here is a picture of colored shapes on a white background. At first glance, the arrangement of shapes looks very casual. But see how some of them curve around in a spiral, like the shell of a snail?

To make this picture, Henri Matisse (pronounced *Ma-teece*), first painted his colors on separate sheets of paper, then he cut them out and stuck them down on a white background, just as a collage is made.

The colors are as carefully arranged as the shapes. Look how that big blue shape touches its opposite color, orange. Can you see a yellow shape next to purple? And how many red and green shapes can you see together?

If you still think *The Snail* looks casual, paint some sheets of paper; then try tossing the colored shapes onto the floor. You will see that Matisse did not make his picture in this way!

Perspective: Magic . . .   Methods . . .

Do you feel you could walk into some pictures, like Alice in Lewis Carroll's book, *Through the Looking Glass*? This is because the painters of these pictures use a visual method called perspective. For hundreds of years, artists in Europe developed ways to create the impression that their pictures were not flat boards or canvases. They set out to make their pictures look like windows through which you could see into the distance.

Do you remember that when you describe a "perspective" picture, the part that seems to be nearest the front is called the foreground? The most distant part is called the background, and the part in between is the middle ground? It is like looking inside a toy theater with actors, scenery, and a backdrop.

background
      middle ground
           foreground

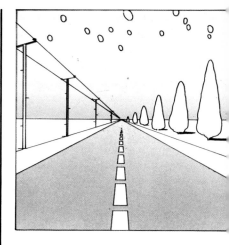

Lines
Painters create the effect of distance in five ways:
1. They use lines which would all meet at one point if you joined them up. (This is called linear perspective.)

Texture
4. They make textures like grass, fur, or stony ground clear and recognizable in the foreground, but they make them fuzzy in the distance (textural perspective).

36

Size

2. They draw the things in the foreground bigger than the same sort of things in the middle ground or background (perspective of scale).

Things in front

3. They draw people or things so that the ones in the foreground block out part of the things behind them (perspective of contour).

Hold up your thumb against some distant buildings. Which is bigger: your thumb or the buildings? You *know* that houses are bigger, so this drawing says they must be a long way away.

Now see how your own eyes can play tricks on you! Here are two lines: ab and cd. Which looks longer?

Now take a ruler and measure each line.

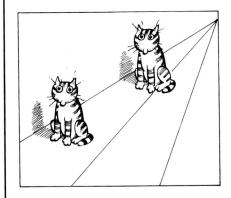

Pale distances

5. They use paler, bluer colors for things in the distance (aerial perspective).

However, some painters use only one or two of these methods, and some do not use any at all.

Now add them together

How many of the five perspective tricks are included in this drawing?

Have a look at other pictures in this book and see if you can spot how many of the five ways each painter uses.

Which cat is bigger and which is smaller? Use your ruler to check the answer. Can you see why your eyes tricked you? (A clue: it is something to do with the way the lines are drawn.)

Take a Line for a Walk

The artist, Paul Klee, once described drawing as taking a line for a walk. See the line "walking" across the bottom of these pages? It begins as a slow, gentle curve; then it does a nervous little zigzag. It becomes a thick, wavy line, then a hard, sharp line, bending and turning in all directions. Suddenly, it hops into tiny energetic dots, and eventually, it wanders vaguely off the page. This line seems to have a personality of its own.

Start with a doodle

When you doodle with a pencil, you build lines up into patterns. Try it and see! Is your doodle made up of geometric, coiled, or spiraled patterns – or some other kind?

If you look carefully, you will begin to notice patterns in lots of different things.

Lines as lines

Can you find here a straight line, a curved line, a wavy line, a jagged line, and a dotted line? Which ones are thick and which are thin, and which line is both thick and thin?

Psychologists say they can tell a lot about a person's character and mood by studying the way he or she doodles, even with uncomplicated lines like these.

Lines as boundaries

You can create a line without actually drawing one, if you bring two colors together. Here is a boundary "line" between orange and blue.

Outlines and edges

Drawn boundary lines look quite different. Color can be used to create an edge, too. Edges made with colors can be smooth, or rough, or blurred.

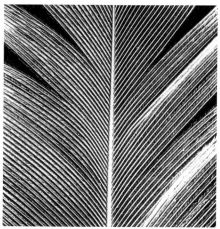

See how the thin lines of this feather fan out from a strong central branch? Leaves have branch patterns, too. Look for spirals in pinecones, cobwebs, and shells. Or make a print of the coils in your fingertip.

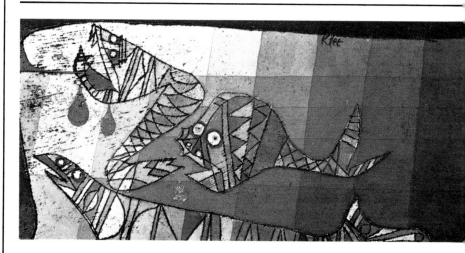

Something is fishy

Look at this detail from Klee's painting, *Sinbad the Sailor*. You can see the outlines of the fish, but the artist also used lines to make clever patterns. Do you think that the spiky lines suggest the scaly skin of fish?

Now look closely. Can you find Klee's signature on his painting? Klee signed his name in splintery lines to suit his picture.

Lines as shapes

A line may describe a flat, two-dimensional shape, like this circle. Or it may describe a three-dimensional shape, like the six-sided cube above.

All kinds of shapes

See how many shapes you can draw in both two and three dimensions. Here are some suggestions: stars, clouds, cones, triangles, and rectangles.

Lines as pictures

You can use words to describe something – say, a fish – or you can use lines. But when you make patterns, you are enjoying the lines themselves.

All kinds of patterns

Patterns can be random – like those in a butterfly's wing, or geometric – like this group of hexagons (six-sided shapes) that make up a honeycomb.

Painful lines

See how Picasso repeated short, sharp lines in *Guernica*? The lines "sound" like the rat-a-tat-tat of a machine gun, and they affect our nerves in the same way.

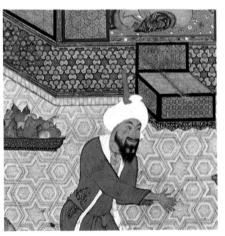

Beautiful geometry

In *The Physicians' Duel*, Aqa Mirak made beautiful patterns from lines. Can you pick out tiny circles, hexagons, and six-sided stars in the picture?

Find the lines

Look back at the pictures in this book and see which artists have been interested in drawing lines. Both Klee's *Sinbad the Sailor* and Picasso's *Guernica* are almost entirely made up of lines. What about Crivelli's picture, *The Annunciation*? Look at this picture upside down to see the pattern of lines best.

Think of the big tree in Avercamp's picture, *A Winter Scene with Skaters*. The lines of the branches also make a very delicate pattern.

Remember Titian's portrait of *A Man in Blue*? There are no strong lines in it at all. But can you see where Titian created boundary lines between the blue sleeve and the dark cloak? Can you also find some boundary lines of color in *Bathers at Asnières*?

There is one painting where you can hardly find any lines at all. The artist was more interested in the quality of light than in drawing lines. Can you find this picture? (There is a bridge in it, but even the lines of the bridge are vague.)

Shut your eyes and draw

First, get a piece of paper and a pencil. Then, shut your eyes and "take a line for a walk" across the paper. It is just the same as doodling. Now, open your eyes, and see what your line looks like. How many words can you think of to describe the different lines you have drawn?

Light and Shade

Using light and shadow is one of the most powerful ways to create a mood of drama or mystery in a painting.

The kind of pictures that spark your imagination or start you daydreaming often have a marvelous quality of light. It might be gentle daylight, or a dramatic shaft of sunlight, or the mysterious glint of candlelight among shadows.

Gaining our attention

Sometimes, artists use light to hold our attention. Look at Klee's painting, *Sinbad the Sailor*, on pages 16–17. See how the pale squares make a shaft of light that draws your eyes to the center of the picture?

Light and shadow

You probably know that at 12 o'clock – when the sun is overhead – things cast hardly any shadow. But when light shines on an object from any other direction, a shadow is always cast.

Some painters use shadow to make people or things look solid or three-dimensional. Remember the shadows in the big blue sleeve on page 26? Or the shadows that show the muscles of the horse in the picture, *The Cowboy*?

Other artists are not interested in using light and shadow. Take another look at the rest of the pictures in this book to see which painters use light and shadow and which ones do not.

front

behind

right

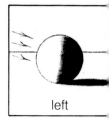
left

Making shadows

You can experiment with light. If you put a lamp or a flashlight in front of any object, you will see: a shadow is cast behind it. Light from behind = shadow in front.

Light from one side = shadow on the opposite side.

(Sometimes, painters show the sun, or a candle, or a lamp. But usually they "suggest" the direction of the light.)

Shadowy grays

Scribble heavily with a pencil, then more lightly, to get a few shades of gray. Or draw crisscross lines in pencil, or lots of dots or stripes. Now see how many gray shades you can make by mixing different amounts of black and white paint together.

Shadowy colors

When you add black or white to a color, you change its tone. Try mixing up different amounts of white with blue. Then mix black with blue in varying amounts.

How many light tones and dark tones can you make by mixing?

a

b

above   below

Light from directly above = almost invisible shadow below. Light from below = shadow above.

Now experiment by lighting a person's face in several ways.

Follow the light
Without the shadows, this tomato would look very flat. How can you tell that the light is shining from the right? Now look at the three drawings below. Can you find the position of the light shining on each of these people? The answers are on page 46.

c

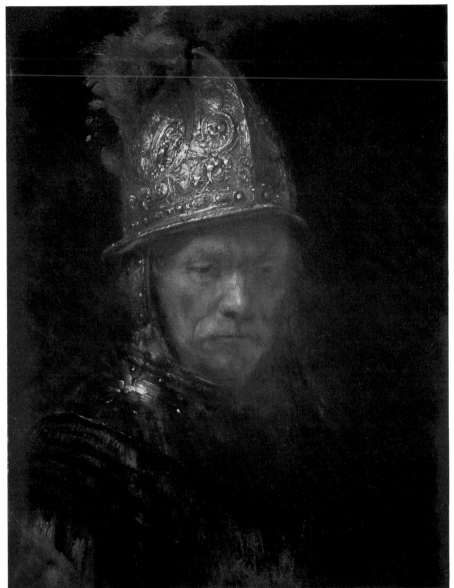

The Man with the Gold Helmet by Rembrandt van Rijn painted about 1654 size: 2 ft. 2 in. × 1 ft. 8 in.

Look at this man's magnificent gold helmet. It is bathed in glowing light, while the rest of the picture is sunk in dim reflections and deep shadows. Rembrandt used candlelight to draw our eyes to details in the picture. See how the light picks up the tips of those feathers and the glitter of a gold shoulder-buckle? It also flickers across the man's face, just catching the expression in his eyes. Can you work out where Rembrandt put his candle to paint this man's portrait?

Feeling without Touching

Have you ever described something you have touched as "hard," "soft," or "smooth?" These words tell people about the texture of that thing. Everything has some kind of texture. Gravel feels rough, and sand feels silky. Fried eggs are slippery, and breakfast cereal is crunchy.

Sometimes you can sense how something feels simply by looking at it. You probably would never touch an owl or a porcupine, but you can *see* what those creatures would feel like. You would never actually touch a painting either, but you can often sense how things in the picture – or even the paint itself – would feel.

When you see a painting printed in a book, you cannot always get a sense of texture. But if you go to a gallery, you could look out for all the pictures that make you want to reach out and touch them.

Swirling brushstrokes

Look at this picture of a starry night. See how the paint spirals, twists, and rolls over the canvas? And how the trees on the left "flame" with texture? The real painting makes your fingers almost itch to touch it.

The artist, Vincent Van Gogh (pronounced *van Go*), loved both the texture of paint and the textures in nature. See how the surface of his canvas is lumpy? Look at the swirls of yellow paint – like giant pinwheels – racing across the sky. The cypress tree looks thick and snaky, too.

Here is Van Gogh's drawing of the same scene. Its surface is flat. But the vigorous lines tell you about the textures in the trees and fields. And, just like the painting, the stars glow brightly.

Make a collage

Why not make a collage using natural texture? You could collect fallen leaves, bark, ferns, or grasses. Choose different colors and textures, and arrange them on a sheet of white paper. Paste everything down with white glue. If you glue leaves or ferns on top of each other, you can get a raised surface texture, just as Van Gogh did with paint. You can also make textured collages with sandpaper and broken eggshells or scraps of velvet and satin.

Rub a texture on paper

Place a sheet of paper on any textured surface and simply scribble over it with a soft pencil. You could rub over a brick, a coin, or a knotty piece of a wooden floor. You will see lots of different textures and patterns. Or rub across the backs of leaves – then you can look at shapes as well as at textures in nature.

The Starry Night
by Vincent van Gogh
painted 1889
size: 2 ft. 5 in. × 3 ft.

As smooth as satin

Here is part of the portrait of the man in blue. You can sense, just by looking, how soft and shiny that big sleeve would be. The surface of Titian's picture, though, is very smooth. You can't "feel" the texture of paint as you can when you see Van Gogh's picture of *The Starry Night*.

Notice the difference between Titian's soft curves and the distinct lines in the drawing by Van Gogh. Titian did not use line to show texture. Instead, Titian makes you "feel" the richness of the satin sleeve by showing you how it softly folds and crinkles as the man bends his arm. See the shadows in the curves of the glossy material? Imagine how cool and smooth the satin would feel. Titian used light and shadow to tell you about texture.

Putting it All Together

If a hundred artists painted the same subject, you would see a hundred different pictures. That is because every good artist thinks and feels differently about a subject. A painter may be inspired by an idea, but his real challenge is deciding the best way to put it across. The first decision he makes is how to arrange everything in his painting. The proper word for the arrangement of things in a picture is composition. To help him compose a picture, an artist has color, line, the five methods of perspective, light, and texture. He might use one of these things, or a few, or even all of them! When he had made his decisions, he puts all the parts of his picture together on the canvas.

Balance
Here is one way of arranging things in a picture. Everything seems to be well-balanced in this drawing. You might think that such an arrangement is a bit obvious, but an artist can very easily focus your attention by putting things right in the middle of the picture.

Oops!
Another artist might want you to feel nervous and uneasy. He can do this by making the picture unbalanced. Of course, the canvas would not *actually* tip over like this! But it gives you the idea of a painter who is deliberately crowding things on one side in a disturbing way.

Variations on a theme
The inspiration, the vision, the great idea – that is a painter's starting point. The challenge is how to put it on canvas. What if artists were drawing a snail? One artist may long to capture the wonders of nature. He might draw our attention to the roundness and beautiful markings of a snail, describing the tiny creature in exact and minute detail.

Another painter may be inspired by the thought of the dangerous life a snail leads, always afraid that a bird is going to pounce on it. (Luckily, snails probably are unaware of their fate.) This artist might create a moody, dream-like atmosphere – a world of huge leaves and dark shadows where the snail must constantly watch out with alert, stalky eyes.

Harmony

Some pictures have a pleasing rhythm and harmony, just as music does. This drawing makes us feel comfortable and calm because of its harmonious composition. The figures are still grouped on one side of the picture, but now they are balanced by the tree.

Two portraits

An artist may decide to make someone look important by putting him right in the middle of the canvas. Now look at the drawing that shows the person slightly to the left. A painter might do this to make us feel puzzled or curious about someone's character.

Compose things yourself

Ask if you can have a bulletin board to hang in your room. Then think about arranging your pictures and other treasures on it. Arranging a wall panel is a bit like arranging things in a painting. When you look at your blank board, imagine you are an artist facing a blank canvas. Where to begin is quite a problem, even if you already have an idea of how your panel should look. First, place everything on the floor. Shuffle the things around to get a pleasing arrangement before you pin them into place. You will find that there is a lot to consider: the sizes and shapes, colors, the spaces to leave in between, and where you want to put your favorite picture.

Have you ever noticed how tiny and slow-moving a snail is? An artist may find that this appeals to his imagination and sense of humor. He might paint a picture that shows a funny little snail trying to get somewhere in a hurry.

Yet, another painter could look at a snail and be fascinated by its spiral shell, starting small and getting larger.

Can you imagine which parts of composition (perspective, line, color, light, and texture) each of these imaginary painters might use? Or where they might put the snail in their pictures?

Now look back to see how Matisse arranged his colorful shapes in a snail-like spiral. The white spaces in his picture are just as carefully arranged as the shapes themselves.

What To Do Next

This book has been about noticing and enjoying pictures. But the original painting – the one actually created by the artist – is ten times more exciting than any reproduction. That is why going to an art gallery or museum is such an adventure.

Visiting art galleries

Find out where your nearest picture gallery is. You might already have been there on a school trip. But it is much more fun to go alone or with a friend. That way, you have lots of time to stop and stare. And you can get really close to a painting that interests you, to see *exactly* how the artist has put his paint on the canvas. Some galleries also have special children's groups.

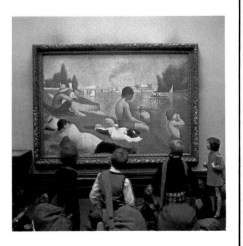

Keep looking!

Try going back on another day to look at a favorite painting again. You will notice so much more the second time. Picasso once said that a picture only lives through the person who is looking at it. Part of the thrill of looking at pictures is finding something new each time. Why not look back at the pictures in this book?

Chase a subject

Hunt for pictures that show one of your favorite subjects – perhaps musical instruments, machines, cats or dogs, or mythical animals such as dragons and unicorns. Ask yourself which picture is the funniest, the strangest, the most exciting or appealing, and how each one is different.

Make some sketches

If you are not too shy about other people looking, take a notebook and pencil and sketch the things that interest you. You could start a notebook of drawings of dresses or unusual hats. If you are interested in buildings, you could do the same with window shapes, or chimneys, or rooftops.

Use your view finder

Sometimes, there is so much to look at in a gallery that it is hard to concentrate on one picture. And very often, big old fashioned frames trick you into thinking that the pictures are dull and old fashioned, too.

Make a view finder as shown on pages 4–5, and use it to blot out the frame and all other pictures. Hold the view finder up and look through the hole. Then move backward or forward until all you can see is the picture.

Discover more

If you have enjoyed a particular picture in this book, why not read about the artist? Many of the great painters were like explorers, because they discovered new ways to put across their ideas. Find out who discovered how perspective works, for instance, or who first used oil paints.

Starting a collection

Another idea is to make your own "gallery" at home.

Start by cutting out pictures from magazines. Or buy postcards and posters. Trade cards from galleries with friends or relatives in another town or country.

Pin your collection to a wall panel like the one shown on page 45. Try to use straight pins – they are better than thumbtacks because they do not cover up so much of the picture. After a while, you get used to looking at the same things, so keep changing your collection. If you could have one of the paintings shown in this book for your collection, which would you choose?

Understanding a picture

How do you look at a picture that is different from anything you have ever seen? At first glance, you may not like it or understand it. Perhaps the painter uses a "language" you do not know, as if someone were speaking to you in a foreign tongue. Try looking at the picture again and again until you begin to absorb the colors, the patterns, and the shapes. Look at other pictures by the same artist, and read a bit about his life. Paintings are often easier to understand when you know how an artist thinks and what things interest him.

Be yourself!

Never feel that something is wrong if you dislike a famous painting – everyone in the world reacts differently to pictures. If you go on looking and discovering, you will find some pictures that you can enjoy forever.

In the detail quiz on page 30, the answers are: 1d; 2f; 3b; 4c; 5a; 6e.

Remember the palette quiz on page 34? Here are the answers: 1b; 2f; 3d; 4c; 5a; 6e.

In the shadow quiz on page 41, the answers are: a, right; b, below; c, above.

Glossary

acrylic paint A paint in which the **medium** is acrylic resin, a type of shiny thermoplastic.

background The distant part of a painting, representing what lies behind objects in the **foreground**.

binder Something that makes things stick together.

canvas A piece of firm, closely-woven cloth backed or framed and used as a surface for painting.

collage Artistic **composition** made of various materials (paper, cloth, etc.) glued on a surface.

composition The arrangement of objects into the proper proportion to each other.

detail A part of a whole; the small elements of a work of art.

foreground The part of a painting nearest to and in front of the person looking at it.

illustration A picture (in a book, for example) designed to explain or to decorate the text.

matt Having a smooth, even surface, free from gloss.

medium A substance, for example, water or oil, with which **pigment** is mixed to make it a liquid.

middle ground The part of a picture between the **background** and the **foreground**.

monogram A character or figure formed with two or more initials of a person's name combined in a single design.

opaque The quality of not letting light pass through; not **transparent**.

palette Thin oval or oblong board, with a hole near one edge through which the thumb is inserted. A painter holds and mixes **pigments** on his palette.

pattern An artistic design or arrangement of form.

perspective The representation on a surface of the relationship of objects in space as they might appear to the eye.

pigment A substance that gives black, white, or a color to other materials. Powdered pigments are mixed with a **medium** and a **binder** to make paint.

pointillism The theory or practice of applying small strokes or dots of color to a surface; seen from a distance, the colors blend together.

portrait A painting of a person, especially one of his or her face.

primary color The colors from which all other colors are derived; in painting, red, yellow, and blue.

print A reproduction of an original work of art made by a photomechanical process. Prints are sometimes made in limited, numbered quantities under the supervision of the artist.

secondary color Color formed by mixing any two **primary colors** in equal proportions.

shade A color produced by a **pigment** containing varying amounts of black.

still life A painting of mostly inanimate objects.

texture The visual or tactile surface characteristics of a work of art.

transparent Fine or sheer enough to be seen through.

Bibliography

Canaday, John. *Mainstreams of Modern Art*. Holt, Rinehart & Winston (New York, 1981).

Cumming, Robert. *Just Look: A Book About Paintings*. Scribner (New York, 1980).

Gombrich, Ernst H. *The Story of Art*. Prentice-Hall (Englewood Cliffs, 1985).

Gregory, Clive and Sue Lyon, eds. *Great Artists of the Western World*. 20 vols. Marshall Cavendish Corporation (Freeport, 1987 and 1988).

Holme, Bryan. *Enchanted World: The Magic of Pictures*. Oxford University Press (New York, 1979).

Janson, Horst W. and Dora J. H. *History of Art for Young People*. Harry N. Abrams (New York, 1986).

Richardson, Edgar P. *A Short History of Painting in America*. Harper & Row (New York, 1963).

Weiss, Harvey. *Pencil, Pen, and Brush*. Scholastic Inc. (New York, 1974).

Index

Picture Credits

Illustrations
Malcolm Livingstone.
Photographs
p 5 Rodney Todd-White; pp 6–7 Reproduced by Courtesy of the Trustees, the National Gallery, London; pp 8–9 By courtesy of the British Library Board; pp 8–9 AISA/©DACS 1989; Alphabet and Image; p 13 Reproduced by courtesy of the Trustees, the National Gallery, London; pp 14–15 Reproduced by courtesy of the Trustees, the National Gallery, London; pp 16–17 Private collection, Switzerland © DACS 1989, Colorphoto Hinz, Basel; pp 20–21 Reproduced by courtesy of the Trustees, the National Gallery, London © DACS 1989; p 22 Reproduced by courtesy of the Trustees, the National Gallery, London; p 24 Courtesy Amon Carter Museum, Fort Worth; p 25 Reproduced by courtesy of the Trustees, the National Gallery, London; p 26 Reproduced by courtesy of the Trustees, the National Gallery, London; p 28 The National Portrait Gallery, London; pp 32–33 Michael Holford; p 33 By courtesy of the British Library Board; p 35 Tate Gallery, London © DACS 1989; p 38 John Vigurs; p 41 Gemäldegalerie, Staatliche Museen, Berlin; p 42 Kunsthalle Bremen; pp 42–43 Collection, The Museum of Modern Art, New York: acquired through the Lillie P. Bliss Bequest; p 45 Steve Bicknell; p 46 Jerry Tubby; Front cover *Myself: Portrait-Landscape* by Henri Rousseau/National Gallery, Prague.